A NOTE TO THE READER FROM TIM AND CAROL SHEETS

God sent His Son...and the story has never been told better than in this new book by JD Hornbacher. He describes the concept of the Trinity in a fun, easy to understand way for children, and actually, adults are going to like it too! JD has a gift and it is an honor to offer our endorsement for *The Big Goodbye*. You, and the children in your lives, will love this book.

THIS BOOK BELONGS TO:

_____

THE BIG GOODBYE

JD Hornbacher   **Tim Sheets**

DESTINY IMAGE® PUBLISHERS, INC.
PO Box 310, Shippensburg, PA 17257-0310
"Publishing cutting-edge prophetic resources to supernaturally empower the body of Christ"

This book and all other Destiny Image and Destiny Image Fiction books are available at Christian bookstores and distributors worldwide.

For more information on foreign distributors, call 717-532-3040.
Or reach us on the Internet: www.destinyimage.com

ISBN 13 TP: 978-0-7684-7623-1
ISBN 13 EBook: 978-0-7684-7624-8

For Worldwide Distribution, Printed in the USA
1 2 3 4 5 6 / 26 25 24 23

THE BIG GOODBYE

JD Hornbacher   Tim Sheets

On a special day in heaven, a long, long time ago
Jesus packed his suitcase for his trip to earth below.

"Clothes and towel, soap and comb," he listed things he'd need.
Then Papa sauntered in and said, "ALL SET TO DO THE DEED?"

"You bet I am!" the Son exclaimed, then something caught his eyes.
He pulled a box of diapers from his suitcase in surprise.

"Very funny, Spirit!" Jesus shouted with a grin.
"I got you extra padding!" **Spirit giggled, bouncing in.**

"You're gonna be a baby! Just the cutest little tyke.
Crying, laughing, pooping—gasp! I wonder what that's like?"

"I'll tell you when I get there," Jesus said and rolled his eyes.
Then Papa laughed and stepped between. "ENOUGH OF THAT,
YOU GUYS."

"Do you have everything you need?" **asked Spirit in a rush.**
"Socks and shirts, deodorant—you'll need a new toothbrush!"

BAAA!!

"I'll just floss with sheep's wool
right before I go to sleep."
"WELL THEN," **Papa smiled and said,**
"WOULD YOU LIKE A SHEEP?"

Papa laughed as
Jesus put the
lamb inside
the case.
He zipped it
closed, and Spirit
got a strange
look on his face.

"Being raised by humans..
such a strange part of
our plans.
It's weird to think we
made them—now your
life is in their hands."

"What if you get a headache, or fall down and scrape your knee?"
"I'll have my mother, Mary, who will take good care of me."

"What if someone treats you bad and
you have to be brave?"
**"I'll have a brand-new father who
will always keep me safe."**

"But what if Joseph drops you on your head?" **Spirit buzzed.**

"Well then I'll—" **Jesus stopped and turned.**

"Hey yeah, what if he does?"

"JOSEPH IS A CARPENTER WITH
STRONG AND STEADY HANDS.
I PICKED THAT MAN ON PURPOSE,
HE'S IMPORTANT TO OUR PLANS."

"There's going to be risk involved now that he's trading places."

"BUT I KNOW HE'LL GET THROUGH IT ALL
NO MATTER WHAT HE FACES–
SPLINTERS, BLISTERS, MILD FLUS AND VARIOUS DISEASES.
YOU CAN DO IT, RESCUER," **Papa said to Jesus.**

Spirit started dancing, then grabbed Jesus by the shoulders. "Aren't you SO excited??? Hm, I thought that you'd be bolder."

Jesus sighed, "This will be tough, but something we must do." "JUST STAY IN TOUCH." Papa said. "I'M ALWAYS HERE FOR YOU."

"And I will see you down there!"
Spirit said and danced with joy.

"You're coming too?" said Jesus.

"Of course, you silly boy!
Mary's not yet pregnant,
but that's all changing soon.
A little zap from me and
you'll be cozy in her womb!"

"SO THERE YOU GO! THE PLAN IS SET, YOU'VE GOT YOUR CLOTHES AND TOOTHPASTE. LET'S BE OFF, THE TIME HAS COME. JUST DON'T FORGET YOUR SUITCASE."

"Wait," said Jesus, putting down the suitcase by the wall. "Now that I think about it, this makes zero sense at all."

I've got love and purpose, I don't need more things to carry. And a suitcase would be awkward—especially for Mary!"

Spirit chuckled awkwardly, then whispered, "Bless her heart. I'm glad we picked that girl. She's a wonderous work of art."

"PAIN IS NEVER FUNNY."

Papa's voice was firm and gruff.

He walked up to the Son and said,

"You'll find out soon enough.

MY SON, I'M VERY PROUD OF YOU.
WE'RE DOING A GOOD THING."

"Yes, we are!" Spirit cheered.

"It makes me want to sing!"

"Since Adam and Eve hid from us, I've waited for this day.
To give my life and conquer death—it's the only way."

Papa smiled, then hugged his son, and Spirit joined the huddle.
"The thing I'll miss the most," **said Spirit,** "is all our little cuddles."

"This will be the greatest feat the world has ever known.
Soon everyone will see that there's a King upon the Throne!"

"WE'LL SHARE ALL THAT YOU GO THROUGH—
AFTER ALL, WE ARE ALL ONE.
HOLY SPIRIT, GOD THE FATHER,
AND THE RESCUER, GOD'S SON."

Jesus turned and shouted, "See you on the other side!"
As he walked off to his destiny, the others beamed with pride.

"THE KING OF KINGS AND LORD OF LORDS
ARRIVES THROUGH HUMAN BIRTH.
ALL OF HEAVEN'S POWER COME TO
WALK UPON THE EARTH."

"TWO REALITIES, NOW ONE," **said Papa,** "MERGED INTO A CHILD."
"Buckle up, humanity, cuz things are getting wild!"

"THE GREATEST RISK, THE
BOLDEST PLAN,
AND NOW IT'S COMING TRUE.
A BABY BORN IN BETHLEHEM
IS MAKING ALL THINGS NEW.

"Let's go tell the angels! Man, they're gonna lose their feathers!"
Spirit bounced excitedly and clapped his hands together.

"I can't wait to see Jesus' chubby baby face!"
"BUT FIRST," SAID PAPA, "GRAB THAT SHEEP HE LEFT IN THE SUITCASE."

BAAA!!

THE END

(but really, just the beginning...)

TALK ABOUT IT!

1. Did you ever imagine God, Jesus, and Holy Spirit talking together? Do you think They really joke around sometimes, or do you think They just talk seriously?

2. The Father, Son, and Spirit are three parts of the same God. Is that confusing? Why?

3. Does the book make you think about Heaven being real? Does it make you think Heaven might be more fun than you thought?

4. Why did Jesus leave Heaven to go to earth?

5. What did Papa mean when He said Jesus would find out about pain?

6. Have you ever considered that Jesus might have experienced splinters, blisters, or maybe a cold while on earth? Do you think He experienced things like that?

7. Spirit thought it would be kind of strange for Jesus to be raised by humans. Why?

8. **God said He picked Joseph and Mary especially, to be Jesus' human parents. Do you think God has a purpose, a plan, for your life? Can you imagine what it might be?**

9. **Why did God refer to Jesus as Rescuer? Jesus came to rescue all of us, including YOU! Have you accepted Jesus into your heart?**

10. **Papa God said He would always be there for Jesus. Do you know He's always there for you too? How can you know God better?**

JD HORNBACHER

lives in Alberta, Canada, with his wife and three kids. He is a family pastor and a media producer, and he is obsessed with Jesus, family, church, and comic books. JD's secret is that he would much rather hang out with kids than with adults, because kids are way more interesting and they appreciate his random stories.

TIM SHEETS

is an apostle, pastor of The Oasis Church in Middletown, Ohio, founder of Awakening Now Prayer Network, and author. He travels extensively throughout the United States, Canada, and other nations, carrying his heart and vision for awakening and reformation. He teaches and ministers in conferences, Bible colleges, seminars, and churches, releasing the authority of the believer and an anointing for signs, wonders, and miracles.

From
Tim Sheets & JD Hornbacher

What would you do if you met your Guardian Angel?

That's exactly what happens when Zoe asks for God's help to deal with the school bully, Talia. But Zoe gets more than she expected when her angel, Joph, takes her on an incredible mission to battle the demon, Fearmonger. On this assignment, she must gather the pieces of the Armor of God so she can remove the fear-seeds planted by Fearmonger.

But can she face her hidden fears and greatest mistakes? Can she trust God and make the ultimate choice to bring freedom to herself, her loved ones, and even her worst enemy?

This hilarious and impactful story will answer tough questions about God, while empowering you to live with strength and confidence. On this exciting journey, you will discover how partnering with God's angel army can bring victory to your life and Kingdom transformation to the world around you!

"What did you think angels did?" Joph asked.
"I don't know," I admitted. "Like, sit on clouds and play harps all day."
Joph rolled his eyes. "Well, I do play a mean harp, but no. We are defending you, secretly and unseen, fighting against evil forces."
I scrunched my nose in confusion. "When? How? I never see any of that happen1"
"I know." Joph struck a karate pose. "We're like ninjas. With feathers."

Purchase your copy wherever books are sold